By Rev. Angela Cosner

An Instrument of His Love

Unless otherwise indicated, all scripture references are take from the King James Version.

Because these are true faith stories, only first names of some of the persons have been used. The names are not important; God's work in the lives of ordinary people is-----and that is the reason for re-telling the events and sharing the stories in this book. May they be an inspiration to all of us.

International Standard Book Number 0-87012-652-0
Library of Congress Control Number 2001116132
Printed in the United States of America
Copyright © 2000 by Angela Cosner and Kathy Johnson
Burlington, WV
All Rights Reserved
2000

Camera-ready material provided.

McClain Printing Company
212 Main Street
Parsons, WV 26287
http://McClainPrinting.com

Preface

    The day Pastor Angie walked into our church, my faith began to grow and my life began to change. She walked to the elements' table in front of the sanctuary and placed a bottle of pop on the corner of it. She turned to face the congregation, smiled, and asked us, "Is this bottle half empty or half full?" And for the next hour, I never yawned or squirmed or looked at the clock. I knew---we all knew---that we had someone very special in our midst who radiated God's love and came to serve His people with all her heart and soul.

    Pastor Angie is one of those remarkable people who makes a lasting impression on anyone she meets. As you read the stories of faith she has shared, you will realize many things. The most impressive thing to me----as I listened to the stories and have watched her as she works---is the way she humbles herself before the Lord. Her greatest desire is to be obedient to God, and her greatest strength is her humility. She doesn't have to preach that; she demonstrates it: no frills or airs-----just pure faith.

    Not long ago, Pastor Angie was seriously ill, as the first chapter of the book describes. One morning service during her children's sermon, she wanted the children to know about healing and anointing. She talked to them and answered their questions, then she asked for their help. Gathering the children around her, she told them to get a dab of oil on their finger, and she asked them to touch her with it. She bowed and kneeled amongst them--- all that could be seen was her head with dozens of little hands touching her--- and they prayed. Such an anointing came over our church! Members who were there worshipping that day can still feel the touch and see her humbling herself before the Lord, among His children, asking them to pray **with** her and **for** her. What a beautiful message for all to see and experience!

I guess I can best describe Pastor Angie by using the comments of one of her students in a nursing assistant class. (She is also a registered nurse.) Her student wrote of her, "Angie has a way of making people want to learn....If Angie were a high school teacher, I am positive the school would have fewer dropouts. But since she is not, she can only touch the lives of the people she meets. I don't believe I've ever met someone as sincere and giving to others as Angie."

That is what this book is all about----leading people to Him, being a servant of God, radiating His love, allowing God to guide our lives, fully trusting Him to lead us where we are supposed to be, desiring---above all else---to serve Him and be obedient to Him. This book is not to praise Pastor Angie or her ministry, but to show how God can work through each of us if we seek to be and allow ourselves to be---as she does----*An Instrument of His Love.*

Kathy Johnson
Burlington, WV

An Instrument of His Love

1. "I Have More For You To Do"
2. "God Has A Calling For All Our Lives"
3. "I Just Want To Be Obedient, God"
4. "We're Gonna Love Him Back To Life"
5. "Witches and Warlocks, But God Is The Victor"
6. "God Puts Us Where He Wants Us"
7. "Yes, There Is Life After Death"
8. "You Got Your Miracle, Kathy"
9. "God Promises To Meet Our Needs"
10. "Frogs, Friends, and Families"
11. "God Has A Pager, Too"
12. "I Love You, But I Don't Want To"
13. "They Have To Let Me Go"
14. "I Am Willing, Lord, But I Am Not Perfect"
15. "Seeding Cherries And Sorting Fears"
16. "We Are Called To Help, Not To Judge"
17. "God Is Calling, But Are You Listening?"

"I Have More for You to Do"

It took an out-of-body experience and a little peek at Heaven before I realized that I was missing what He was telling me. The Lord wanted me to slow down and listen---really listen---to what He was saying to me.

Some of that day I remember clearly, some of it is more like a dream, and a little of it I don't remember at all. But the part I remember most clearly—being in the tunnel, hearing the beautiful music, and having the Lord speak to me—is what has driven me to share the faith stories in this book. It was one of the unfinished tasks the Lord told me to complete when He sent me back.

I guess one of the first warning signs that my life was about to change came as I was sitting in my recliner reading, and I started feeling short of breath. The shortness of breath continued, and I started getting chest pains. I am a registered nurse as well as a licensed pastor, so I tried everything that I had been taught to relieve the pain; nothing worked. I decided to call a friend in the church—an EMT—to bring the equipment to my house to run an EKG, but I instructed her not to bring the ambulance. I didn't want to alarm anyone, especially some of my elder parishioners who lived near me.

The first EKG strip was okay, but the pain continued so we ran another. That one showed me that we had a problem! At that point, the pain was so bad that I could not get up from the couch, so I was taken to the hospital by ambulance. My mother had died of heart disease when I was in my early twenties, and I began to wonder while the medic worked on me as we sped to the hospital if it wasn't my time to go.

I remember feeling, as we had entered the month of October, that I was on a treadmill that I couldn't get off. I had let myself get so caught up in doing too much, and I just felt like my life was out of my control. Even when I was rushed to the hospital and put in intensive care, I felt like I needed to be doing something, taking care of something, going somewhere.

As I lay in intensive care, thinking about all that was happening to me, I began to feel myself "distancing" from those in the room. I could hear the technician talking to me; I could hear a pastor friend who was there laughing and talking to me. I could feel myself nodding and smiling, but at the same time I continued to feel like I was "distancing" myself from them. I was just about to begin **another** journey!

The technician and my pastor friend left. I looked at the monitor, and my blood pressure was only thirty. The top number on the monitor wasn't reading at all, so I reached for the nursing button and pressed it. It was at that point that my real journey began!

I knew that my spirit was leaving my body. It is hard to explain how it felt. It was like a tugging within my body—a shifting, like a mini-earthquake within me. After that, I saw a light, and that was it for this body! I was going home! I remember looking back at my body lying there in the bed and thinking, "Boy, she looks tired." I was watching from above when two of my parishioners came into the room. They both told me later I had a fixed stare and wasn't responding to them at all.

At that time I was truly **on** my journey; I was out of that room—and I mean "out" out. Many of my elder parishioners have experienced the same thing and have described it to me. Like them, I was in a tunnel, but I was stuck there. I could see back, and I could see the golden light ahead. I could feel the Peace, and I could hear the music, but I couldn't go any further. I didn't get to walk in the grass, either, or talk to people there like others have described to me.

That is when it happened: God spoke to me. He truly spoke to me. He didn't give me a choice of whether I wanted to go further or come back. He told me I **had** to come back. He told me that I needed to look back over my life.

I remember looking back and seeing different things that I had started but not completed. I saw many things that I needed to finish. He told me that I was to write a book of faith to help other people. He let me see back over all the experiences of faith that I have seen and been a part of in my life and in my ministry, even back into my mother's womb. There are a lot of people that find themselves in the same situations that I had been experiencing and ones that I had witnessed, and they have no hope. I looked back over all the different areas of my life and each one shares a different story of faith. They all tell the story of how God can reach down and be in the midst of the storm and comfort and rescue us from our troubles if we let Him. It was then that my mission became very clear to me.

I knew my mission, but I needed a spokesperson, and——just like every other miracle of faith——God takes care of everything. He sent me a person with a gift of writing, a love of writing, to work with me on this project. Actually, He had nudged us before to do this project----and both of us realized it---but we never followed up on it. A couple of summers before my illness, this person——a parishioner of mine—- and I were talking, and the idea of a book came up. She asked me to work with her to compile a book of some stories that I had begun to share with her. I agreed, but we just never got around to it. I guess the Lord got tired of waiting and decided to tell us a little more clearly what to do.

When I was rushed to the hospital, the prayer chain was begun in my church. On the morning I was rushed to intensive care, Kathy (my writer-to-be) was sitting by the phone------ready to do some work on her computer. The call came about me, and she said she immediately began to pray. Up to this point, she and I were more like acquaintances than friends. We talked often ——mostly by phone——-because she does the monthly newsletter at my church, but we never spent time together to allow ourselves to develop a friendship. The morning when she got the call and had prayed, she had an experience that began the link—the true friendship—that brought us together to work on this book. It was no doubt the Lord's work and His intention that a partnership for Him result—for me to tell the stories of faith that I have witnessed or experienced, and for her to use her talents to write them for others to hear and be encouraged by them.

As I had looked back over all the areas of my life, and God was showing me these things during my journey, one thing I knew was that I had to get this book written and published. I really struggled with that. Maybe one of the struggles is that I don't feel really comfortable writing a lot, and I try to avoid it as much as I can.

My lifelong goal has always been to serve the Lord and to share the stories of faith that I knew. I remember feeling called as a child to serve the Lord. I spent my time pretending to be a preacher in my grandparents' church when most young children were playing school.

Kathy's background and training is in English and journalism, and she has done freelance writing all her life. Her goal has always been to write a book. Look at how this miracle had begun to develop!

That morning, as soon as she stopped praying for my recovery and healing, she said the Lord spoke to her as she sat down at her computer. He said to her, "This message is for Angie," and she just turned to face the computer and began to type. The words He gave her just began to pour onto the screen as she typed. Being a Christian rather new in her faith and just beginning to seek the Lord, nothing like this had ever happened to her before. She was very "rattled" by this, and she called her friend Susie, another parishioner who had been visiting me, and told her what had happened. Amazingly, Kathy had no knowledge or clue of the journey---the out-of-body experience---I had begun in the hospital as she had been praying.

She called our mutual friend Susie to explain what had happened. Though she didn't understand it all just yet, and she really didn't understand why or how this had all taken place, Kathy knew that what the Lord had given her and she had typed had to be given to me. When I got the message and I was coherent enough to listen and understand it, it really spoke to me. I knew God was telling me what He wanted me to do with my life. So He put me together with this wonderful friend who has the gift of journalism and a calling upon her life. It is only together working as a team, with the gift that she has and the calling and the push that He has put upon my life of sharing the experiences of faith, that we can put the word out and share these stories that the Lord has provided.

Anyway, God sent me back. He wouldn't let me continue on my journey. Needless to say, I was a little disappointed. I could see the light and hear the beautiful music. I didn't see God, but I could hear His voice and feel the warmth and the glow all around. I knew that just beyond the glow—that Heavenly light-- were my parents, and boy I was ready!! But He sent me back!

When I woke up, I was in the hospital bed. It was early in the morning, and I turned on the light to call the nurse. I wanted to take a shower. I felt alive, and I felt a surge of energy! It was a different kind of energy, though. It wasn't the kind that had been driving me before. It was a spirit-driven energy that told me to get on with God's work.

So finally the nurse let me take a shower, and I kept asking the rest of the day about going home. By nine o'clock that night, I was out of there.

I had felt a desperate need the Friday before all this happened to begin the tapes for this book. I began the first tape, knowing that something was going to happen. I just knew it, and I knew I was supposed to begin this book.

The realization that I had been with God and experiencing God the presence of Him sent me back with a sense of peace about me. It renewed my sense of humor and allowed me to start enjoying life more. I was faced with the idea of human "being" and not human "doing." I knew I had to relax and just be myself and be the child of God that He intended, to allow myself to be renewed each day by His presence and His blessing. Life had become a chore for me. I was ready to lay it down. But He had renewed me and sent me back!!

"But they that wait upon the Lord
shall renew their strength;
they shall mount up with wings as eagles;
they shall run, and not be weary;
and they shall walk and not be faint."
Isaiah 40:31

"God Has A Calling For All Our Lives"

I know that I have been called to the ministry since I was thirteen years old. That's when I began sharing scriptures and these experiences. This journey began for me really when I was nine years old, and I was diagnosed with leukemia. I was so pale and tired and weak all the time. My mom would give me this tonic to take to try to help me. But I was **so** tired. It got to the point that my dad would meet me at the bus stop to carry my books and sometimes literally carry me home. But I didn't want anyone to know he did that, so he had to wait in the bus shed or down around the turn. Sometimes, though, I just did not have the energy to move. By that time they knew that something **had** to be done.

They did everything they could do, so they decided they needed help with it and took me to the doctor for blood work. It was then that I was diagnosed with childhood leukemia, and I started the treatments. Like every kid, I dreaded the needles and shots. I got so thin and weak from the treatments that my parents literally carried me around. But I had such a thirst for knowledge that I insisted that my homework be sent home so I could try to keep up with the other children at school.

It was a difficult time for me. No one wants to be bald, especially a little girl, but I **was** from the treatments. And with my last name being Mick, I was often called Mickey Mouse. It was a lonely, frightening experience because there were thoughts of death, and this was at a time when the childhood diseases---or really any disease—were not as openly talked about and accepted as they are now, so I suffered and felt the cruelty and ridicule of the other children. We were not a rich family anyway, and my parents didn't have much medical knowledge, so there was very little support or encouragement for me or for them. They became very discouraged, and it was very trying and scary. It was a very bleak time for me.

Up until that time, we---mostly I----were attending a little church near my house where my grandparents had donated land to have a church built. I had this little Sunday school teacher that would come to the house and get me if I didn't show up each Sunday. I don't know who kept her class while she came and got me, but it was important to her that I be there. She was a stern little lady. She would show up at the door and say, "Where's Angie?" It didn't matter if I was still in my nightgown or what, I had to go!! I remember throwing a dress over my nightgown more than once and going with her. I knew it was useless to argue.

There were times, though, that I would stay back intentionally to make her come and get me. I think I did that so my parents would have to have contact with her in hopes that they would have the desire to go to church, too.

But God uses all things to glorify Him, and I think that is why the illness came upon me. By then I had taken all the treatments the doctors felt that I could have, and they felt there was nothing more they could do for me. I had lost so much weight and was so weak that they felt more treatments were useless. They felt that it was totally up to God, and my body needed time to just restore itself. I remember that day so well! They told my parents that I would probably never live to be a teenager and that they should take me home and enjoy me as much as they could while they had me.

At that time I was ten years old, so I could understand what the doctor was saying, and I was not liking what I was hearing. It brought such a fear, and so I had many questions as we traveled home that day about death and dying, what that would mean, and what that would feel like. My dad was very quiet in the automobile, but my mom shared about the eternal life and how peaceful and comforting it is there. She told me there was nothing to fear. And I knew from my mother's teachings that day that Jesus would come and take me and that I would not have to fear going to heaven alone, but that it would be an exciting trip with Him.

I remember being taken home and being carried to the couch. They went to the kitchen and had a little muffled conversation. Then my mother came in with a Bible. I didn't even know she read the Bible. But she had been because it was worn from having been read. I think it had been her mom's.

She looked up the story about the woman with the issues of blood. That story so impressed them that they wanted to go to church NOW! They didn't want to wait until Sunday, they wanted to go NOW! So my sister took us to a tent revival at Seneca Rocks. They patiently waited in the back of the tent until the minister asked for prayer needs, and my mom said she had a daughter that was in the need of prayer. So they carried me up to the altar, and they all gathered around and laid hands on the people in front of them. Those in the front were touching me, so it was one huge chain of people praying. The evangelist anointed me, and I can still smell the oily smell of the tent and the smell of the freshly cut grass where it had been mowed to put the tent up.

    I didn't get up and run around and instantly have hair, but I felt a warmth wash over my body that night---a kind of healing warmth. It starts at the top of your head and comes down over your body, and it is just awesome. I just felt so close to Jesus. Even being a young child, I knew that Jesus would meet my need. I knew that whatever the healing would be---whether He was going to take me home to be with Him or if He chose to give me more time here on this earth, either way it would be just fine. It was months before I was able to do normal things again, but my appetite came back immediately. But we left the revival that night with the gift healing and of salvation, for I received the Savior's touch and my father had given his life to Christ. I really believe that this was the full purpose of my illness, that God would be glorified through it.

    Up until this time, our entire household was usually in turmoil. The environment was not good. My dad worked away during the week, and he did a lot of drinking. So when he came home on weekends, he continued to drink, and he could be a very violent man. There were many times he would get the gun out and shoot at things, terrifying the whole family. Everyone was very thankful when he would fall asleep, and it would finally be peaceful for a while.

One of the things that I discovered as a child was that when I was suffering from leukemia, I couldn't run and get away from him and his rage and loudness. But I could sing, so I would sit and sing church songs. It was just like Saul in the Bible when he was being tormented by the evil spirit. When David would play the harp, Saul would feel peace and be comforted. That's how it was with my father. I would sit there singing, and such a peace would come over him to hear the church songs. His rage would be calmed, and he would go off into a sleep. It was at this point that I began to see God touch him through the songs before he really recognized the scriptures or Jesus as his Savior. It was the songs that brought peace to his spirit.

As my disease worsened and my dad started to take time off from work to go with us to the doctor's visits, my dad began to soften as he saw me go through the treatments. I began to see God work in my dad's life. I began to see tears of compassion in my dad's eyes and concern on my father's face and in his voice. It was through this that the Lord had begun to heal my father, taking away his addiction of alcoholism.

One day after my healing I got a letter from a small church in Whitmer asking me to come and share my story with them. It was exciting for me to have an opportunity to witness to them and to begin answering the call I felt upon my life. I used to sneak over to the church near the house and pretend I was having service there. In those "pretend" services, I had people praising all over that church. I would get behind the pulpit and I would do the whole thing. I would welcome them and ask them to have an open mind and an open heart, and I would go over to the piano and play them a little song. Then I would go back to the pulpit and open the Bible and read the scripture. I would even give the altar call!

Well, I went to Whitmer to speak at the church there. As I spoke on "Miracles for Today," I used the scripture about the lady with the issues of blood. I was only thirteen years old, and I remember feeling nervous as well as excited. There were probably thirty or so people there. At the end of the service, they all came forward at the altar call and wanted prayer.

At the time of my birth, my mother was forty-eight years old. She already had seven children, five girls and two boys. The pregnancy was difficult for her. But God was planting me---this seed of faith---within her and was calling me, I think, even from my mother's womb to do ministry. I believe this because He gave me illnesses at a very young age, and pulled me through those illnesses. Others around me were witnessing the events in my life. They saw God at His work and was saved and blessed by it.

I do know that the Lord heard my mother's cry and answered her by anointing my body with healing. He also anointed me with a calling to go forth, to speak His word, to show His love and compassion, and to remind others that there is healing for those who believe and seek Him. We just need to call upon the Lord and be patient and be quiet before Him. We need to **allow** God to heal us. And He **will do** as He promises!

*"Heal me, O Lord, and I shall be healed;
save me, and I shall be saved:
for thou art my praise."*
Jeremiah 17:14

" I Just Want to Be Obedient, God ..."

I have always had a thirst for knowledge and a dream for education. As a child when I was diagnosed with leukemia, I missed so much school because of my treatments, but I had such a desire for knowledge——to know things and to learn things. I was always reading. The rest of my family wanted to get out of school as quickly as possible, get married and have families, but not me-----I wanted an education. I loved school, and I would cry when I had to miss days. My mother would always say, "I don't understand this. All the other kids were happy when they had to stay home, but it is like a punishment for you because you desire to be there."

I realized as I finished my senior year that if I didn't get loans and scholarships, continuing my education was just not going to happen——it just wasn't going to be possible. And it wasn't. I ended up getting married and having my son. I was to realize that my dream **was** possible in God's time, not in my own.

My dream just wouldn't die. I took some vocational training, and I worked as a nursing assistant at the hospital, then in home health care. I thoroughly loved going into the homes and tending to the physical needs, but I would also do the spiritual care. If I saw that they needed milk or bread, I would remember to take some in with me the next time I visited. I just tried to bring some extra joys into their life, like taking a flower to someone who had probably never gotten one before or some kind of special surprise for them. I just wanted to share the love of God with people. It was wonderful, and I loved it.

During that time, my pastor could sense that God had more of a calling upon my life, and he shared that with me. He shared the gift of prophecy with me, and we put out the fleece, which was a practice in the Bible. As I searched and sought for guidance, I felt that the Lord was leading me to go to nursing school.

So I put out the fleece. I said, "Okay, God, if this is of You, You will give me a sign and let me know definitely that this is from You and not just Satan's way of moving me from where I am comfortable and taking away what gift of ministry that I **do** have."

The first thing I did was go out to Davis and Elkins College and fill out the applications. As I filled out the forms, the office staff told me that they felt it was too late in the year to really be accepted; it just wasn't going to work out for me. School started in August, and this was in May, so time was getting very short. I said, "That's okay. I will just go ahead and fill them out anyway. If I am supposed to go this year, I will. If not, I will go **some** year."

When they realized that I wanted in the nursing program, they told me that I would have to take an entrance exam and asked if I wanted to come back at another time to take it. I decided that I just wanted to get it over with. I told them that I would just pray and take the exam right then. If I passed it, fine. If I didn't, that would be God's way of answering me and telling me that is it not His will.

I went in, and I sat down at the desk to take the exam, praying over it as I did. As I prayed, I picked up my pencil and began the test thinking, "Surely, as hard as this test is, God wants me to stay in home health care and do what I am doing." So I went home, ministered to my home health care patients as I worked, and I waited.....

About three weeks later, I received a letter saying that I was accepted into the nursing program! At that point I was faced with another hurdle, another step of faith that I had to get through-----the financial aid. So I went to the financial aid office and filled out all applications and the forms to apply for money to go to school. They were polite but not encouraging, explaining, "Well, now we have already given all the financial aid for this year, so there probably won't be any available for you."

I said, "Well, if I don't get any this year, that's fine. I can always come another year. I am just trying to be obedient." I filled out the forms anyway, prayed about it, and went on home and gave it no more thought, really. A few weeks later——we're into late June now—I got a letter from the college saying that some students had dropped out and that now there **were** some scholarships available! The remainder could be a student loan, and it wouldn't have to be paid back until after I graduated and was working. Once again, God answered and was showing me that he really wanted me to go on to college and into nursing.

I still struggled with the idea of leaving my comfort zone. I was living close to the minister's family and was settled into my home church, speaking and witnessing there. I was teaching Sunday school and working in a job that I really loved. Now, here I was faced with a real step of faith into the unknown.

The next obstacle soon presented itself: I got a letter saying that I needed $186.46 for registration. Needless to say, I began praying about that letter. No one else knew about this need or this dilemma, and I went to work that day wondering what God had in store for me this time.

One of my patients that I went to see that day lived up on the mountain and out away from any community or real neighbors. She had no phone and was bedfast. She could tell that I had something on my mind that morning. I was sharing with her about how I felt God was trying to move me, but I wanted to make sure that it was God and that I could hear His voice and be obedient to Him. I did not want to be led astray by a desire that I had because I loved to learn, but I wanted to be obedient to Him. So she prayed with me. We prayed that before the day be over that God would show me without a shadow of a doubt that it was His will for me to go to nursing school.

It was about noon that same day, I was at another patient's house in the Lahmansville area, and there was a phone call. It was from a lady in my church who was trying to track me down—to locate me to see what was wrong. I said, "Nothing's wrong, and I assume everything is fine with my son. He's at school."

She said she had been praying and doing her devotions that morning, and God had told her to get out her checkbook and to write me a check for $186.46. She said, "So I know something is wrong, and you are so quiet. You are not one to ask for help. Are you sick? Is your son sick? What is going on?"

At that point, I was crying so much that I couldn't explain, but I told her that I would stop by her house and relate to her what God had just done. Later that day, I explained to her that through her God had answered my prayer——right down to the penny——and that I knew that I was supposed to go on to college. So I packed up, moved, and took that step of faith to attend Davis and Elkins College. That was just the beginning of seeing many miracles revealed to me in my life.

As God sent me out into the health field, he sent with me an idea and a concept of holistic health care. With any and all patients that came into my care——and those that still do—- I not only do a physical assessment, but a spiritual one as well. I had come to realize the need for spiritual healing in my patients. I fully understood that it was vitally important for them to know the Lord as part of their total and long-lasting healing.

God provided, and my dream to go to college was accomplished; I began working at the hospital. The idea of holistic health was planted in me, though. It was constantly on my mind as I tended the needs of my patients. I had one patient that continued to come in with a stomach ulcer. We would have her in and do the IV care, the right exercises, the right medicines and such, and release her. In six to eight months, she would be back.

I did a spiritual assessment with her and realized that she was harboring some unforgiveness and anger toward someone in her family. Once she was able to talk about that, I was able to pray with her and ask God to help heal those feelings and fill her with His peace and love. After that, we did not see her come back to the emergency room. She is just one example of the miracles I began to see in my health care experience. She had finally received a **total** healing, a holistic healing—-and what God sets free is free indeed!!

"And we know that all things work together for good
to them that love God,
to them who are called according to his purpose."
Romans 8:28

"We're Gonna Love Him Back to Life"

We'll just call him Joe. An ambulance delivered him to our hospital from the nursing home. When word came that he was coming, the nursing director at the hospital looked me up and said, "Angie, we've got a patient coming in, and he's <u>yours.</u> He's lifeless; he won't allow himself to eat. He wants to die."

Well, I met Joe at the door as they wheeled him in on the stretcher, and he was the "deadest" alive man I have ever seen. He was so thin! Joe would just lie there completely still with his eyes closed. Unless you were carefully checking to see if he was breathing, you would have thought that he had already passed away.

We took Joe back, put him in his room, and gathered for a staffing. The nursing director told the staff that she had turned Joe's case over to me. So I began by praying about the situation with Joe and what I should do. As our team gathered to develop our strategy, the concept that God gave me to utilize with Joe was that we were going to **love** him back to life—-that this was a man who have given up on life because of who knows what. I didn't know the "because" at that point, but I knew that he had had a very difficult life that had drained him of all hope. It had robbed him of the desire for life.

So my directions in the team meeting were, 'We are going to love him back to life. Anyone and everyone that goes into Joe's room, make sure you **touch** him—touch his hand, touch his head— and say, "Joe, I love you." I want you to **touch** him because human touch is a healing essence.' That even included those who would be cleaning his room. **Everybody** that went into Joe's room was instructed to touch him and say, "Joe, I love you."

We had to put in a feeding tube because he would not eat; he was willing himself to die. He would not talk; he would not open his eyes. He would just lie there very still.

His first surgery was the feeding tube. We put the IV's in and got the feeding tube set up. At first when we would go in to give Joe his feedings, he would just lie there. After a few days, he began to realize what was happening—-the feedings were bringing life back into his body. It was then that he started slapping the feeding tube out of your hand, and the feeding would go all over the place.

Again I called the team together, and I reminded them to have the gift of patience. I told them to expect that to happen and to just bring a change of clothes when they knew they would be feeding Joe. We were all on board with the effort. We continued to let him know that we loved him; we continued to have great patience with him; we continued to feed him.

I was working the evening shift. I went in at seven in the evening and got off at seven the next morning. I would always make sure that I went in to say 'hello' to him. I would say a prayer, and I would tell him that I loved him. Then I would go on and get my nursing reports because those were done at the end of each shift. Then I would do my med rounds.

I always kept Joe for last because I knew I needed to spend more time in his room. Each time I would have to clean up the mess of him knocking the feeding out of my hands, but I continued to share God's word with him and let him know that we loved him.

One night as I was doing this Joe began to show signs of the love of God warming him up inside. I noticed a tear on Joe's cheek, but still no words, still no movement.

One particular night I went in, and I was feeling kind of rushed. I was a little stressed I guess. As I did Joe's feeding, he knocked it out of my hand. It went all over me and all over the floor. I just knelt down beside his bed, and I began to cry out to God. I said, "God, I have done all I know to do for Joe. God, just let him feel Your love, Your Peace——and Father forgive me for the anger that I feel at this time because, Lord, I am just tired this evening; I am just stressed, and it has nothing to do with Joe. So forgive me, Lord, and heal Joe."

As I got up off the floor, he had tears streaming down his cheeks and his eyes were open. I said, "Hello. How are you, Joe? It is good to see you. It is good to see those beautiful sparkling eyes of yours."

Of course, his eyes were sunken back into head and still had that glazed look. He said, "How can you say that you love me, and how can you pray that God forgive me, when you don't even know what I have done?"

I said, "Joe, it doesn't **matter** what **you've** done. It matters what **Jesus Christ** has done. Because Jesus died on the cross so that **all** people could be healed, so that **all** people could be saved, so that **all** people could have eternal life."

Then he began to sob, and he began to share his story, how he had been much younger and had been in a bar room fight and had taken a man's life. He had been put in prison for that. He was released from prison and lived on the street. He didn't go back to his family because he was so ashamed. He felt that he had hurt them so much. All he wanted to do was to die, but for some reason—-as much as he tried—-he couldn't die.

It wasn't God's will and it wasn't Joe's time to die. I shared again about the death of Jesus and about the about the murderer who was on the cross. I told him that just because that murderer believed in Jesus, Jesus told him, "You shall be with me this day in paradise."

I told Joe that God forgave him and that he needed to forgive himself. I asked him if he would like to pray and take a step of faith. Well, that first night he wasn't willing, but he thought about it. A few nights later, as I was feeding him and as I was talking to him, he had his eyes open as was watching me. He reached out and took my hand. That was his first movement, and it was a rigid movement, because he hadn't moved his arms and legs for quite some time. He was going to need a lot of physical therapy.

But he reached out and grabbed my hand. He said, "Do you **really** think that I am forgiven?"

I said, "Yes! Would you like to pray the prayer to receive forgiveness?" He was open to that, and we prayed the Repentance Prayer. I asked God to bring healing and wholeness into his life along with the gift of salvation.

He smiled. He cried, and I cried. Each day we saw more and more improvement in Joe. He became **quite** a talker. Physical therapy went in and began to work on his arms and his legs to help him be limber and mobile again.

I will never forget when he was able to sit for the first time, when he was able to stand for the first time, when he was able to be in the wheelchair outside his door for the first time. We were all excited. It was like seeing a newborn baby taking all those first steps.

Then one night while I was sharing the Word of God with Joe, I asked him if maybe he would like to get in touch with his family. He said, "Oh no, I can't do that. I have shamed them. I am sure they're very angry with me. I am sure they would **never** want to see me."

I said, "How do we know if we haven't asked? So if you give me a name, I will do some checking and see if I can't find some numbers. At least we could **ask.**"

After praying about it, he decided that I could do some checking. I started doing some research and came up with some names. I made some phone calls and found out that Joe's wife was still alive as was his children. They were very excited to hear that Joe, too, was alive and well and that he wanted to see them.

So I set up a date and a time for them to come to the hospital for this family reunion. Well, Joe was very nervous about it, but we all kept him in prayer and continued to encourage him as the day of the reunion drew near.

As the family came that night, I went in the room first and prayed with Joe. I went out to get them, and they went in Joe's room. I stayed there just to make sure there was going to be peace and that there were not going to be a lot of angry words said or anyone would be hurt. But as soon as they walked into the room, they walked over to the bed and began to weep. Joe began to weep, and his wife reached down and gave him a big hug. They just clung to each other. The children all just gathered around them.

I excused myself and went out to let them have their family time and their private time. When they needed me, they sent for me, and I went back in. We had a closing prayer to that family reunion. It was a wonderful, wonderful experience because when Joe left, he didn't go back to a nursing home. He didn't go back and live under some bridge. Joe left and went home with his **family**, with his wife and his children. And Joe left **walking.**

Of course, you know the hospital policy that requires patients to be taken to the car in a wheelchair, but Joe left with the ability **to walk**. Joe left with the ability **to love**. Joe left **forgiven** and **born-again** in Jesus Christ. The man wheeled in on a stretcher from a nursing home, who was the "deadest" alive man I had ever seen —**wanting** to die, **choosing** to die—was born again of the Water and of the Spirit. Thanks be to God!

*"Therefore if any man be in Christ,
he is a new creature;
old things are passed away;
behold, all things are become new."*
2 Corinthians 5:17

"Witches And Warlocks, But God Is The Victor"

It was during my first appointment that I came face-to-face with the occult. Up to that time, I knew it existed and I believed that people worshipped the devil and fought against God's teaching, but I hadn't seen it first hand or had to deal with it. That all changed pretty quickly when I began to work at my first church.

I came into town like the Avon lady----I went all around town, knocking on all the doors and saying, "Hello, my name is Angie. I am the new minister down the street. Come on out."

I am sure after I left each house, they said, "Okay, she sure is excited. Let's go and see what she can talk about!" When I visited some of the older people, I took flowers or fruit, things like that. Then the youth started gathering and coming to church. We started having youth meetings. I began teaching them about the differences in religions and Bibles and finding out from them what they were exposed to. I was looking for places and areas where I needed to give guidance in their lives through the ministry. Low and behold, I discovered that they had been given books on satanism at school---the books that witches use. I was appalled! I mean, they don't even like for us to give out regular Bibles, and here this woman was giving out witches' bibles.

So I gathered up all those books and burned them. The kids brought the satanist bibles in to me, and I explained the danger of having them. We all agreed to get rid of them. They also brought in a lot of CD's and music that they had been listening to, and we burned them along with the witches' bibles.

So this lady in town—who is a licensed witch and had her credentials hanging on the wall and everything---let me know that she did not appreciate me. She sent word to me--- rumors and such—by people that she knew would get the word to me. I am God's servant. I refuse to be intimidated, so I went calling on her at her house.

I knew it was going to be a battle with the devil and her, so I asked a pastor friend of mine to anoint me every time I knew I would have contact with her, every time I had to confront her. My pastor friend understood the occult and the power of anointing and spiritual warfare, and he supported me and anointed me and prayed for me through all of this. We developed a special relationship during this because I knew that he understood and he could see how God was using him **and** me as partners in this battle. I tried to let him know exactly where I was and what I was doing at all times when I had any dealings with the satanists, and I would call him when I was out of danger, when my contact was over and I was away from them.

I let this lady—this witch—know that the youth had to make a choice and they chose life; they chose Christ. She and her warlock friends decided that they were going to scare me enough to leave. They were determined to get rid of me.

That church was never locked. The congregation and the church leaders liked it to be open to travelers or for people to come in and pray. The satanists knew that, so I began to find animals that had been sacrificed in there. I found pigeons and doves and things like that. At this point, the congregation was not aware of what was going on. I would get to church early before anyone would be there for service and did my best to get rid of whatever I needed to before others arrived.

One Sunday morning the lady that cleaned the church went in early to do some things and found a snake. She came running out of the church and went down the road to get one of the neighbors to kill it. Well, he did the deed and hung the snake on the fence. The people that came to service that day saw it, and it was then that they became aware of what was going on. I told them that there was a spiritual war going on, and I told them that they would probably see more signs of it. But I told them not to be afraid because God is all powerful, and He would not allow any harm to come to them. I asked the elders of the church to come forward that day and to anoint our church---the dwelling itself. And then I asked the elders to go outside with me while the rest of the congregation was singing hymns and praising inside and to anoint the cornerstones of the church. Then we just praised God, and there was such a peace there—such a wonderful peace. You could just feel the presence of God.

Well, there was a certain lady in the community who had not been attending church. I had visited her home to invite her to come to worship with us, but as of yet she had not been attending. This particular day she did come to church, and she came forward and asked for anointing and I prayed with her. There was such a joy and celebration when she did—she cried; I cried; we hugged, and she hugged everybody at the church! It was such a sweet victory for Jesus!!!

Well, about three or four days later, things started happening to her. I got this call—this panicked call from her husband. At first, what happened was she would be fine one minute, then out cold on the floor the next. They would rush her to the emergency room but couldn't find anything wrong with her. By the time she'd get to the hospital, she would be okay, and they would bring her back home. That happened over and over.

Then her husband called and asked me to come out and talk with them. He felt that something had a bondage over her life, that something had roots into her life was controlling her and had a bondage over her. So I was anointed and prayed for God's guidance, and I was on my way.

When I got to the house, I found that she was totally blind---couldn't see at all. So I began to pray and anoint her. I asked her husband to stay with us, and I anointed him. We just continued to pray and trust God for guidance.

As I prayed and just waited on God for direction, He gave me a word of discernment. When He did, I knew this problem was connected somehow to a box, and I asked her about it. I said, "Somehow, this whole thing is connected to a box. Does that make any sense to you?" So she told me that she had a box out in her camper that had been her mother's. When her mother had passed away, she had been so grieved and so angry that she didn't even open the box; she didn't even know what was in it. So we send her husband out to retrieve it for us, wondering what in the world we were going to find.

When he brought the box in, I carefully opened it and started taking the objects out. I started describing to her what was inside as I gently lifted each item from the box. One of the first things we came across was a certificate of her mother's, and I began to understand the situation: she had been a licensed, practicing witch. We found her spell book; her bible; her crystal-----all the things that she used to practice her witchcraft were there. I knew immediately that to solve the problem that she faced, we really needed to destroy every one of the items. The existence of the box was an attempt to pass those things and those beliefs and those practices on to the next generation—her. It apparently had been okay that she didn't pick up her mother's ministry----the actual task of practicing it---- but she had gone entirely against it by accepting Christ and beginning to serve Him. Without even realizing it, she had broken the promise of what they had vowed that she would be and what she would do.

So I said, "Can you think back to when you were a little kid?" And she could. "Can you think back to a service being held when you were taken forward and lifted up?" Yes, she could remember that. So we knew that in her childhood she **had** been given to the devil to be one of satan's children.

The task of destroying that bondage was to begin! We decided to take the contents of the box out to a barrel to burn them. I told the husband, "Now I am going to be inside with your wife because I don't know what is going to happen when you start burning these things. But you **have** to get rid of these things."

So we prayed and denounced that promise to uphold the ministry of Satan, and the husband began his task. We didn't realize just how hard that would be. He said he took gallons of gasoline and poured on that stuff, and it just would not burn. He said it was awful. And he said when it did start to burn, it had a horrible smell to it.

As he was burning and trying to destroy that evil influence of the past, I was in with his wife praying and singing and reading scripture and continuing to focus on God. As soon as the things were burned----when that bondage was destroyed----- her sight was restored!

All the experiences that I had been exposed to before this had prepared me to face and battle this black magic. It was a horrible experience. I must admit, there were times that my husband and I would ask ourselves, "Do we want to do this anymore?" There were threats made against me continually and things put in the church.

I worked and traveled late at night sometimes, and one night something did almost happen to me. It was late, and it was dark. The satanists knew enough about my travels to know when I was coming into town and when I was leaving. They made it a point to keep track of me. I had been warned not to stop if anything looked like an accident. I was told if that happened to go on and call back to send help if it was needed. I was not to stop anywhere that wasn't well-lighted and to always pay attention to what was going on around me. Many people feared for my safety.

One night as I was driving home there was a truck pulled halfway across the road in front of me. I knew instinctively that it was trouble, so I started praying, "Oh, Lord, what do I do?" I slowed down as I got closer. I thought, "Either I am going to have to make a U-turn, or I am going to have to stop." So I kept saying, "Oh, Lord, what do I do?" I remember saying the third time, "Oh, God, please give me an answer." At the point where I knew I had to do something, I noticed a dirt road on the right. I had no idea where that dirt road was going to take me, and I didn't remember ever seeing it before, but I hit it as fast as I could. When I did, it took me down around the knoll and back up and on the road I had been on. That was my answer—God had taken care of me. I was on my way again, and the danger was behind me! It reminded me that I would be safe from their attempts to harm me or scare me as long as I trusted and serve Our Lord. He is indeed my refuge and my strength!

"The Lord is my light and my salvation;
whom shall I fear?
the Lord is the strength of my life;
of whom shall I be afraid?
Though an host should encamp against me;
my heart shall not fear;
though war should rise against me,
in this I will be confident."
Psalm 27: 1,3

"God Puts Us Where He Wants Us"

  I had served in my first appointment for six years. We witnessed one church going from just thirteen elderly parishioners attending to more than eighty, with several young families joining and worshipping with us. We witnessed and were privileged to be part of a revival, and we celebrated a breaking free from a cult and from witchcraft in one of the churches. What glorious victories!

  But I knew that my time there was getting short. There came a time that I just knew God was preparing me to move on into another ministry. As He planted that seed of understanding in me and it began to grow, I started to look at the newspapers for the job postings. One day I came across a posting for a chaplain at the Burlington Children's Home in Burlington, WV. I looked at the requirements for the job and knew that I did not have the education or the credentials they were looking for. But the thought of that job stayed with me---it stayed on my heart and continued to be on my shoulders. I saw another posting for a nurse at a boys' center in the area, also. So I applied for that position and interviewed for it. That job was not for me, though. I knew that I wanted to work with the young people not only in a medical role but in a counseling role as well. That facility wanted just basic nursing, so I continued to pray for guidance as to what I was supposed to do. The ad for the children's home kept running in the paper, so I prepared my resume, prayed over it, and mailed it. Once again, I put out the fleece for God's will to be done with it.

Within about a week or so, I heard from the agency, and they wanted me to come in for an interview. As I prayed about it, I felt like this really was not going to happen. But I felt like the interview would be good practice and a good experience. So I went for the interview, and it went really well. I was interviewed by four people that day. I clearly recall one of the questions that day. They asked, "If a person isn't ready to receive God's word, what would you do about it?"

I answered by using a metaphor of something that they could easily understand. The Burlington Children's Home is known for its Apple Harvest Festival. Tens of thousands of people pour into the tiny community of Burlington each year to take part and enjoy the festivities, as well as raise money to support the campus and its activities. I knew the answer they needed, so I explained it this way: "If you would go in May to get the apples for the Apple Harvest instead of in September and put them through the peeler and cook them and process them into apple butter, you would ruin the entire process. It would be a disaster. You couldn't force them to be ready because it would be out of God's will. It would be the same with someone who isn't ready to receive or hear God's word."

They all seemed to look at each other and smile. So I left, and they went over my credentials. I had told them that as of yet I didn't have the qualifications that they were seeking. I explained that during the summer I would be completing my fifth year course of study at Duke University, and I would be completing what I needed to do. I would be receiving my certification and ordination within the next year.

A week or so passed, and I got a phone call from the vice-president of residential care. He told me that the job was mine. He said, "When would you like to start?" I told him that I had to go away for five weeks of schooling, but he told me he wanted me to start before then. He went on to say that it would be an educational training session and the campus would benefit, so they would pay me as I received the schooling that I needed. I thought, "My goodness, Lord, how can this be? They want to pay me as I get the training! What is this, God?"

But I still said, "No. I have to have the weekend to pray about it." And so I took it to the altar at both of the churches that I served, and I prayed. I just knew when I looked back over the congregation and saw families sitting together, mothers and fathers with their children, people eager to hear God's word, that I was supposed to go where there were children who had not heard the Word and did not have the love of parents to assist them in growing in the Lord.

So I called a PPR council (Pastor-Parish Relations) meeting and discussed it with the council. I told them what God had put on my heart. There were many tears, but they said they knew that when God spoke, I had to move. They knew I had to be obedient, even though they would miss me terribly and honestly hated to see me go.

So I called the agency back and told them that I had prayed and fasted about it, and that I knew that I was supposed to come to Burlington. So I became the chaplain on campus, and completed the education **after** the fact, to have the position I have now---assisting the children to receive the forgiveness, the love and wholeness, and help build the trust in their lives that they so much need.

One of my most treasured memories of the campus so far is of a young resident who was in care and whose greatest desire was to have a family. Isn't it everyone's desire to have a family---a mom and dad, brothers and sisters, a home to live in, the same bed to sleep in each night, pictures on your wall, stuffed animals on your table? This young girl would pray the same prayer every Christian ed class. She always prayed to have a family, some mom and dad out there who would take her in and let her be their child.

We continued to pray this prayer as the young girl worked the program. She began to go out into volunteer home settings and foster care settings, and she continued to pray and seek God. We got her out into a home, and God added His blessings; it just seem to work in this home. I'll never forget the Apple Harvest where this young child came running up to me and said, "Pastor Angie, Pastor Angie, guess what I am getting for Christmas!!"

I said, "I don't kno-o-o-w."

She said, "I am getting adopted!"

So this young girl had her prayer answered. After a couple years of every Monday evening closing every Christian ed class praying the same prayer, her prayer was answered: "Dear Lord, send me a family---

a mom and a dad--- to love me and some brothers and sisters." Now this young girl has that and is growing into a young lady, so mature. She remembers those prayers and how God **did** answer them.

God is there in the midst of any and all storms. God is there when there seems to be no hope. He will answer, and He will send special people into our lives to love and fill up those voids---to fill in where the losses and emptinesses are.

I have seen God change so many lives. When I close my eyes and envision the ministry at the home, I just see Jesus using my body as His instrument, as His temple. It is a special ministry. It is a difficult one because it pulls at your heart strings to see so many broken lives and so many tears and the dark side. You have to wonder how a gift so precious as a child that was given by God can be so misused and abused, broken and neglected. The scripture says, "Unto us a child is born, and unto us a child is given." I praise God that Jesus came to build back the lives, to put the pieces back together, to give them a future, to give them hope." I am truly thankful that I can be a little part of that healing and growing and mending.

"Trust in the Lord with all thine heart;
and lean not unto thine own understanding.
In all thy ways acknowledege him,
and he shall direct thy paths."
Proverbs 3: 5,6

"Yes, There Is Life After Death!"

Harry was a parishioner in my first appointment. I was given Harry's name at church. He didn't attend church---not just my church or any church, really---and I was given his name as someone to visit in the community.

When I went to see Harry that first day, he was sitting out on the porch watching a groundhog out in the field. So I just sat out on the porch with him, and we talked about the groundhog. I shared a little bit about where I was from and what church I was serving in the community. The next time I visited, Harry offered me some lemonade and invited me in. During a later visit, he began to really talk with me and to share some of the concerns of his life that had made him bitter.

Harry shared a little about himself, that his wife had died several years before and that he had children---two daughters and two sons. They were all adults and living out on their own. Through some family misunderstanding or disagreement, they had really been at odds and did not get along well with each other. He was very concerned about that. Harry was a little man, and he seemed lonesome to me— little and lonesome, I thought, as he talked to me that day.

It was just a few weeks after that visit that Harry became ill. He was put in the hospital and was diagnosed with a fast-growing type of cancer. The doctors removed a part of his intestines, and then another part. Finally, he had had so many surgeries of the abdomen and intestines that the doctors could no longer suture his stomach. They just used a binder to hold him together and would open him up to do what was called an intestinal wash, just to keep the infection down, knowing that there was no earthly healing for Harry.

Harry was on morphine for the pain, and I spoke with him about Christ. He accepted Christ as his personal savior. He was baptized, and he really believed that Jesus would return and take him home with Him. And on three such occasions, Jesus did just that!

The first time I was called to the hospital, they told me it wouldn't be long for Harry—that he was dying. I got there, and his blood pressure left, his pulse left. We thought that Harry was gone.

I got on my knees beside his bed and began to pray the Lord's Prayer. In the midst of the prayer, I felt a hand touch my head. I looked up, and it was Harry; his eyes were open.

I looked up and said, "Harry, your vitals were completely gone. What did you experience?"

He told me that he felt his spirit leaving his body. He explained how he felt he was out of his body, looking down at the room. He shared how he left the room and went into a tunnel. He told me that he got to the end of that tunnel and saw the bright light, the warmth and the peace, and the beautiful music. But he came back!

I said, "Harry, why did you come back? Why?"

He said, "Oh, but my children, Angie, my children. There is so much hurt among my children. Once I die, they will never get together as family again. I really need God to heal my children."

Well, as the children would come to visit, I would continue to assess and talk with them and pray with them. I tried to be a buffer between them to help them come to terms with whatever it was that made them so angry with each other.

In the midst of this, Harry had a second experience with death. He lost all vitals again. This time he described actually being through the tunnel and into the Peace. He said he was in a green pasture. He said there was this river or stream, and he called it Jordan. On the other side of Jordan, he could see his wife. He said there was such love and such peace there. He said he sat down on that grassy bank beside of Jordan, and he said he talked with Jesus. Jesus told him he could stay, that he had suffered enough. But Harry said, "I need to return for my children. For my children's sake, please let me return." So, again, Harry came back.

It was at this point that I realized that my elder was suffering and suffering and the children weren't doing anything about their broken relationship. So even though I wasn't really their minister, I felt that I really needed to intervene and to try to bring healing into that relationship. So I called them all into a waiting room and shut the door. I explained to them about the health care of their dad and how there was nothing left here on Earth that we could do. I explained how he had had two wonderful experiences of going on, of seeing the Peace, of feeling the Peace, and of talking with God, but that he fought to come back because he felt they would never be a family if he left because of some sort of hurt or misunderstanding between them.

I explained about the degree of pain that their father was in and about the amount of love that he must have for each of them. I explained that he was fighting to stay here, trapped in this physical body full of pain and disease, when he could be with God and his wife on the other side of Jordan.

The children began to cry and open up, and they began to share. They began to apologize and talk to one another. I led them in a prayer; then I asked them to please try to work on their problems and communicate, and to then meet me in their father's room.

They did just that. As they met me in the room, they gathered around the foot of their father's bed. As they did, they began to tell their father that they had been talking, and that they were going to be working on those problems. They had forgiven one another. It was going to take time, but they were going to have open communication. They were going to intentionally focus on working with each other and being a family. Then the youngest said, "Now, Dad, we give you permission to go on to be with Mom and with Jesus."

We gathered in a prayer circle. As we prayed, we ask God's peace and God's comfort to be upon the children. We asked God to be with Harry and that God's will be complete, and that total healing be upon the family. We no sooner said "Amen" than Harry looked at me, he winked, and he grinned. He raised his hand to wave good-bye, then closed his eyes, and crossed the Jordan as He went to be with God.

We all have difficulties from one time to another in our life, but when we are willing to be open and communicate with one another, that's when the true love of God can intervene. God has a set time and a set place for each of us. We need to prepare our hearts and our minds for that time.

"Let all bitterness, and wrath, and anger,
and clamor, and evil speaking
be put away from you, will all malice.
And be ye kind one to another,
tenderhearted, forgiving one another,
even as God for Christ's sake hath forgiven you."
Ephesians 4: 31,32

"You Got Your Miracle, Kathy"

She told me that she was working on the monthly newsletter that she publishes for our church, and she felt like the Lord placed the word "miracle" on her heart. It seemed odd to her, but she really gave it little thought. Everything she started to type, though, dealt with the workings of a miracle. The word was so impressed on her mind that she even designed the children's page around the idea of "miracle."

A week or so later, she had some medical tests run to determine the reason for fatigue and chest pains that she had been experiencing. While in that process, she also had a mammogram done. To our surprise and disbelief, the mammogram detected an abnormality. A follow-up sonogram confirmed the findings, and she was referred to a surgeon.

She requested a surgeon that friends of hers in our church had seen, a man who prayed with his patients before surgery and seemed to be a fellow Christian. She really wouldn't let herself believe that there was a problem. Why should she? She had always been healthy. Though we could clearly see the growth on the x-ray as we looked at it and talked about it, she was sure it was a cyst and nothing to worry about. As her pastor **and** a registered nurse, I knew it could be more serious than any of us wanted to believe.

The surgeon had second thoughts, too. "Up to about an inch," he said, "we usually don't worry." Hers? "About an inch."

She decided, after hearing her options, to have the mass removed and biopsied as soon as possible, so surgery was scheduled for the following week. I went to the exam with her and listened as he discussed it with her. During the exam, Dr. Chisholm mentioned that he could not detect the lump when he examined her. That seemed unusual to her, but she really didn't question the comment.

We were discussing his comment and lots of other things on the way home, as we usually do. I felt the excitement of a miracle happening and smiled at her. "It's gone, Kathy," I told her.

"What do you mean, 'It's gone'"?

"It's gone," I repeated. "I prayed for a healing for you, and I think it is gone. I was watching a healing program and the minister said, 'If you seek a healing miracle for someone, place your hands on mine on the screen and pray with me for them.' I did and I felt the Lord's touch. I am telling you, it's gone. And the surgeon said he couldn't find it when he examined you, didn't he?" Then I asked her bluntly and directly, "Are **you** praying for a healing?"

" Should I?" she asked. As soon as she said that, I saw a look of doubt and fear cross her face.

"Yes, definitely," I told her. "God **does** answer prayers."

I knew she had begun to think about why she hadn't asked for a miracle and why she was still hesitant to do so, and we began talking about it. "Pastor Angie," she told me later as we talked about it, "I feel so blessed in my life as it is now, is there a point where God says that someone has enough? I feel guilty asking for more." She said that she realized that she never does ask anything for herself. She always prays for others, and she tries to give to others and do for others, but she seldom—if ever—-asks God's blessings for herself.

So she began to pray about her surgery, not for a healing, but just to turn it over to the Lord. For the first time in her entire life, she said she felt like she truly turned a problem over to God. She said, "Lord, I just put it in your hands. Whatever comes, just give me the wisdom and courage to do what I should do. It's yours now." Being a new Christian with a growing faith, that was quite a step for her!!

We started to wonder if the mass **was** gone, or if we were hoping for the best. Were all of the puzzle pieces that seem to point to a miracle just coincidence, or was a real miracle unfolding in her life?

We all began to pray harder. The more we prayed, the more relaxed and at ease she seemed to feel. She told me that she honestly felt that whatever came from this, it would be okay. In the meantime, she kept thinking of a friend that had a desperate need, a need that she felt was far greater than hers. One day she was doing errands to help organize an effort for her friend that would solve monumental problems for the family and ease the pressures for them. As she was working to help them, she felt an overwhelming burden to pray that her efforts **would** succeed and be a blessing to the family. As she was driving along doing the errands and talking to people who were in a position to help solve her friend's problems, she told me that she was praying fervently: "Lord," she must have said aloud, "please just open the hearts of everyone I contact to let them feel the need and want to help. Please, Lord, just allow me to be able to do this for Connie and her family. You and I know how desperately she needs this."

As she drove and prayed so earnestly, she said she feel the most awesome touch just wash over her body, and the Lord told her, "**You** have a need, too." She said she could only describe it as a "cleansing" feeling, starting at the top of her head and washing over her entire body. She said she felt like she tingled all over, and the feeling lasted for miles as she drove home.

I knew the Lord had been working in her life for several months, but this was something that she had never experienced before. This was awesome!!

I'm sure she couldn't wait to get home to tell somebody!! She told her husband, our friend Susie, me, and anyone that she knew would listen and understand. She wanted to share her excitement!! **Was** a miracle unfolding? Was this another piece of the puzzle? "Lord," she admitted, "if this is a miracle you are working on for me, it will loosen my tongue to witness for you!"

That Sunday in church, we all felt the presence of God so strongly in the service. During service she looked transformed and enveloped in a shroud of love and glory. Our friend Susie, our church organist, told me later. "I looked back during service and Kathy was just glowing. I wanted to jump up and shout, 'It's gone. I know it's gone!'" I told her that I had felt the same thing.

Kathy began to talk about what was happening and to wonder-----could it really be gone? Had a miracle taken place? She said she surely did feel different!! Susie and I both encouraged her to get another mammogram, but she was embarrassed to ask. She knew it was an unusual request to have a second mammogram so soon.

She began to pray about that. I know that she really struggled with the feeling of wanting another mammogram and the indecision she felt about asking for one. Finally she called and, as she had anticipated, the secretary told her that she doubted very seriously if the doctor would approve another mammogram. The insurance would certainly not pay, and it just isn't normally done.

She continued to struggle with wanting to know and not feeling comfortable about asking. She gets up early each morning to read a devotional and pray, and she said this particular morning she felt the Lord was telling her that she really should have another mammogram. She said she understood that part, but she didn't understand why she was so angry and frustrated by the thought of it? God gave her that answer, too. She realized that she was embarrassed to explain to the doctor or nurse that she felt the Lord had healed her. She was allowing the devil to betray her. He was saying to her, "If it isn't true, Kathy, you will look like an idiot. They will be laughing at you when you leave. Don't you know that?"

She was learning a lesson in obedience!! After struggling and praying even more, she called the surgeon's office again. I'm sure she told herself, "I am just trying to be obedient."

"Look, I came to Dr. Chisholm because he is a Christian, and I am, too. And here's the deal," she told them. She explained all the events that had happened to her and how she felt touched by the Lord. She told the nurse that she had felt healed, and **that's** why she wanted another mammogram

As soon as she did that, she said she felt the burden was lifted from her. She realized at that point that for the first time in her life she had openly spoken about faith and God without embarrassment and had tried to be obedient to Him.

"Let me pull your chart," the nurse told her pleasantly. Then she explained that there **would** be another mammogram just before the procedure begins to pinpoint the mass for the surgeon, and that should ease her mind.

"What if they don't find anything?" she asked. "What will happen with the surgery?"

"Then it will stop right there, and **everyone** will be happy," the nurse told her.

The weekend dragged for all of us---especially Kathy---and the day for the surgery arrived. We prayed for her and just tried to be supportive and encouraging. She still didn't have fear, but she was getting anxious: she just wanted to know what was happening to her.

The second mammogram was performed first thing that morning in preparation for the surgery. I asked the nurse if I could go back to wait with her and pray with her. The lump was still there and clearly visible. The strange thing was she didn't seem to be disappointed. "It's all His," she reminded me.

Her husband Bill, her sister Laura, our friend Susie, and I waited as she had the procedure. When the surgeon came to us to report on her condition, we knew it was not good news. "She is resting comfortably," is all he would say. "We are waiting for the lab report."

We all sat there, silently, in shock and disbelief. We knew what he **hadn't** said was a problem!! And yet I felt a victory in her faith; I knew it was going to be okay, and I refused to doubt it.

"May I go back and talk with the doctor?" I asked her husband.

"Go ahead," he told me numbly. "You would know what to ask him."

I went to the desk and asked if the doctor was still on the floor. "He's in room three," the nurse told me, so I went to wait for him.

"Doctor," I said as he came by me, "I am a registered nurse **and** this woman's pastor, and you will simply have to give us more information than you just provided. If I am to counsel this family like I should, I need to know what you think about her condition and what is going on."

He looked me squarely in the eye and somberly explained his findings during the surgery: the size, the coloration, the fish-tail shape, and the texture and general appearance. "As a registered nurse, you know exactly what I am telling you," he said. Everything he mentioned to me indicated that the lump was malignant.

"Yes, as a registered nurse, I know exactly what you are telling me, but as this woman's pastor, I am telling you that you are **wrong,**" I told him. "I saw the spirit of God surround this woman in my service, and I **know** you are mistaken!" I explained.

He shrugged his shoulders, and answered softly, "Miracles **do** happen." At that point the phone rang and he said, "That might be the call we are waiting for with the lab report."

He answered the phone and listened intently. As he hung up the phone, I saw tears in his eyes. He looked at me and exclaimed softly, "Praise the Lord! Miracles **do** happen!" I repeated his words then, too, but perhaps a little too loudly! What a celebration when I took the news back to the waiting room!! We hugged and cried and cheered.

When we were able to go into the recovery room to see Kathy, we were all still ashen-faced and shaken, yet excited and full of joy. She didn't realize at the time what we had been through. I went over to the reclining chair where she was resting, knelt down beside her, and whispered, "You got your miracle, Kathy." It was several days later that she fully understood what I meant.

Now with all the check-ups over and she's had time to put this all in perspective, she realizes that she did indeed get her miracle. God didn't remove the lump, as we expected, but he certainly took care of it in his own way! She says she gets out the lab report and reads it often: "Mammography highly suggestive of cancer." Just as frequently, she talks of the all the events that were pieces of God's puzzle as he formulated this miracle, -----and she is thankful for the experience. She had never found it easy to witness to others about God, but now it is hard for her **not** to. She has experienced something so glorious that she just **has** to share. She tells me often of someone she met doing this or doing that and how she was able to witness with her story. Perhaps best of all, she has learned about being obedient to God, despite fear of embarrassment or rejection. When I hear her talk to people about this event in her life, she always ends by saying, "It was a humbling experience, but it truly enriched and changed my life." Since this experience, I have seen her grow in her faith and become a willing witness for the Lord.

I will never forget the first day she was at worship service after her surgery. She could have preached the sermon! She had always been very quiet and rather introverted, but this experience had indeed loosened her tongue for the Lord. She gave a testimony during service, and I could see her just glowing with God's anointing. The experience brought a total healing to her life---physically, spiritually, and emotionally. When she witnesses to people and tells her story, she often says that she has never been happier! Who could believe that a scare with breast cancer could be such a blessing?

God will always take care of our needs, if we trust Him and accept His answer, not just search for our own.

"Trust in the Lord, and do good;
so shalt thou dwell in the land,
and verily thou shalt be fed."
Psalm 37:3

"God Promises To Meet Our Needs"

God sends us special people in our lives to heal the void of lost parents or of a child. I would never have guessed that God was at work providing a miracle for my life as I went off to work that day at the hospice unit of the hospital. My patient was a lady dying of cancer. Her husband was there with her, agonizing in her pain and suffering his own loss as she slipped away day by day.

This couple had no children, no one to help ease the pain and talk with, so I spent my breaks with them. I would share scripture and songs. For her birthday, I took her roses to cheer her and let her know that I really cared about her.

As weeks passed, she went into a coma. Alfred, her husband, appeared hopeless and helpless. On one occasion, I walked into the room and he had his head in his hands and was sobbing. I went over to him, got down on my knees in front of him, and asked him if I could pray for him. I had already prayed earlier with them about God giving the gift of salvation, but this was another chance to pray with him and help him grow in the faith. As I prayed with him, I asked God to bring him a peace because it tells us in John 14 that God goes to prepare a place for us, and He will take us unto Him. I wanted him to know and realize that his wife's journey would not be alone, but that God would enter into that room and get her and take her with Him. If he could find the peace and comfort in that, then he also would feel God's presence when He entered the room to take her.

He was crying out because he felt helpless. He felt there was nothing he could do for his wife at this point, and he had been such a good partner and caretaker. I reminded him that the sense of hearing was the last to go, and I encouraged him to read the book of Psalms to his wife to bring peace and comfort to her in her last days and hours. So each day, he would settle down in the chair with the Bible and his handkerchief, and he would read to her----day in and day out. I would go in and have prayer and sing hymns with them as much as I could during the day. A deep friendship developed between this elderly man and me. A peace and a love of God just enveloped that room. Eventually God **did** return and God **did** take Beatrice home to be with Him.

I was away at a nursing training when I got the call that she had passed away, and Alfred had asked me to come home and preside over the funeral. At that time, I was a lay speaker, and I did not even know if I could do the service. I was honored, but I was scared to death. I had never done a funeral before. So I called one of my mentors, Rev. Kile, and he helped me put together the service. I spoke with a message from the heart, and I sang *Amazing Grace* as part of the service.

My husband, my son, and I adopted this elderly man as a father figure in our lives. He called every day to say hello. He was always ready and eager to travel with me to hospitals, nursing homes, church services, or revivals. He became a spiritual father to me. He filled the void of my lost parents.

We were great fishing buddies. Every year we eagerly waited for stocking season. We challenged each other as to who could catch the largest fish or the most fish. He was my father in every sense of the word. I would run home to him with my confusion or prayer need. He always had a kind, listening ear.

We began to study God's word together. Alfred developed such a thirst for Biblical knowledge. He would read and write down questions to ask me. We spent wonderful times looking and searching for answers together.

He was my prayer warrior and such a support for me in my ministry. He would go to the hospital to visit parishioners with me. He would be there if I was sick and was always willing to do anything he thought he could do to help me. Such a special gift of friendship!!

Each holiday, the passing of a birthday, or something as innocent as a homemade piece of fudge (which he meticulously measured, cooked, and cut into squares) never fails to trigger a wonderful memory that my family and I were blessed to share with him.

One night on the way to a revival service I asked him if I could start calling him "Dad." He said he was so honored for me to do that. Alfred was so gentle and kind in every word and deed. He said that he and his wife had desired and prayed for children, but their son had died at birth. Now, at long last, God had provided him with a daughter.

As he grew older, he would try to prepare me for his passing by sharing the "I am an old man" story. I would never listen to that story because I could not think of a day without him on this side of heaven.

Now that he is gone—as he tried to tell me---God has lifted me and guided me through that valley, too. I know that one day I will see Alfred and all my loved ones again, maybe standing side-by-side, as they wait to welcome me Home. What a celebration that will be!

So, just as God promises, he met both our needs.

He can meet our needs in most unusual ways, **and will**------if we just let Him.

"Those things, which ye have both learned, and received, and heard, and seen in me, do: and the God of peace shall be with you."
Philippians 4: 9

"Friends, Frogs, and Families"

The Lord truly does work in mysterious ways! In my current congregation, the idea of "frogs" has captured everyone's imagination. It has allowed us to reach out to people in miraculous ways and witness to them——using even the quietest members in the congregation.

It all began when I was critically ill for a few months. I was returning from a doctor's appointment with Susie, a parishioner friend, and we stopped at a Wal-Mart on the way home. To relieve some of the stress and just to pass the time, we found the "child" in us taking over and ended up in the toy department. As we walked down through the aisles looking first at this toy then another, we came across some toys that talked and sang. Needless to say, we began to push their buttons and laugh at their antics.

Somewhere in the midst of the toys, we came across a talking Kermit, the large green frog from Sesame Street. At one point, he began to sing, and we began to laugh uncontrollably. Since we were on our way to choir practice that night—and our church choir is a very fun-loving group—we decided to take a mascot with us—and we did!

Choir that night was a little more festive than usual! Kermit was given a place of honor on the organ, facing the congregation, and he became a topic of conversation. This was shortly before Christmas, and the jovial mood of everyone was soon to play a part in this scenario.

As the congregation arrived one morning for service, they found Kermit had donned the festive dress of Santa! He was wearing a Santa suit, smiling as always, and perhaps even a little more talkative. You see, Kermit had begun to add his comments to service. Perhaps the vibration of the organ, the gentle motion of someone walking nearby, perhaps a little nudging from the Lord—who knows?—but Kermit had begun to sing and talk to us nearly every service.

As the days and holidays passed, Kermit would be dressed for the occasion, yet no one would admit to being the tailor. It became a tantalizing mystery to be solved. It sparked good-natured detective work among the choir members. When the mystery couldn't be solved and the tailor couldn't be located among the choir members, it spread to the congregation. What fun it became!! What a topic of conversation......what a neat way to begin talking to someone.....what a neat way for everyone to reach out and enjoy the fun!!

In the meantime, my friend Kathy, with whom I am writing this book, had been to a Christian book store and found another piece to this growing ministry—coffee mugs with frogs that used the image to project the idea of F.R.O.G. ——Fully Rely On God. Well, that just fit perfectly into our happenings! She bought the mugs and all the frog contents as a gift for Susie and me, and that sparked our imagination even more!

We were captivated by that idea.

Shortly after that, I had to go to the hospital for a heart catheterization as a result of my illness. Kathy and Susie both went with me to my appointments and eventually to the catheterization, and that, too, became an event to remember---an opportunity to witness to the heart catheterization unit and to share this growing ministry.

Kathy and Susie, without planning with each other or discussing it, both gave me a small, glow-in-the-dark plastic frog for me to take into surgery that morning. I held them throughout my surgery, and the doctors and nurses all asked about them. Well, we all just had to witness to them and tell them what they represented to us. During the wait for the surgery, the room was filled with laughter and love. The nurses would go get other nurses to come back to our room and laugh with us and hear our story. The doctor, when he came into the room, was drawn into the fellowship and worship---because that is

exactly what it was, fellowship and worship in a most unusual place!! We gave frogs to the nurses that came in and told them to share the story with others. We were escorted to the car when they discharged me, and my nurse was crying and thanking us for witnessing to her! She hugged me goodbye, and I could feel the blessings of the day, even in the aftermath of my surgery.

Since then, the idea continues to grow. We all carry frogs with us in our purse or pocket to use as a witness tool, because we have been able to witness to people in waiting rooms, in restaurants, in department stores----anywhere casual conversation comes into play. We have people ask for them to share with others, and we have had people cry to us after sharing with them because they have been touched by our witness and love and laughter. The frog is a wonderful, tangible reminder to F.R.O.G. (Fully Rely On God) every minute of every day. They glow at us even after the lights are out, reminding us to talk to God and give our thanks. Our church even had a Frog Sunday service, organized by the youth, to worship and praise God's presence in our midst. During most services, the younger children go back to the nursery for their "lesson." On that Sunday, worshippers could have heard a pin drop in the congregation, and every tiny set of eyes and ears were alert and listening to the service. What a glorious day it was, and our church was full and nearly overflowing!!

God wants us to **enjoy** worshipping Him, and He allows us to reach out to others ---young and old alike---with love and joy and fellowship in many unique ways---even with an idea as simple as frogs.

"O sing unto the Lord a new song;
for he hath done marvelous things:"
Psalm 98:1

"God Has A Pager, Too"

He had retired and moved into the area, and had visited different churches around our community. He just happened to visit our church one Sunday. He was kind of amazed and perplexed at the young female pastor who liked to use a lot of stories mixed with humor and metaphors, but had a way of making the message very clear----especially what God was saying to him in particular. He decided that this was the church that he wanted to belong to.

He asked if I would come for a visit, and he gave me the directions to his home. I went, for I welcome the opportunity to visit with parishioners when I get the chance, and we sat and talked. We were sitting around the table, and he wasn't sure that he had completely committed his life to Christ. So we prayed the prayer there around the table and asked for God's true gift of salvation.

He seemed to have such a special fondness for birds, nature, and had such a sense of humor. Shortly after he had started to attend our church, he was diagnosed with terminal cancer. We discussed this. No one knows the "whys" of life. Here he had recently retired and should be enjoying some of the best years of his life, and they were cut short for him. But he did decide in the midst of all that to make the best of it and to enjoy what time he did have. Even though I couldn't help him with the "why," I could help him with the "now." I could help him find the peace and the beauty that God had put in each day for him. I could help him see the blessings that He **was** giving him.

I encouraged him to reach out and make a gratitude journal and look for the blessings in each and every given day. He did that and was very blessed by it.

His cancer progressed very quickly. I visited Stewart after the cancer had really begun to take its toll, and he was still very alert. We had quite a conversation about heaven and what it would be like--- the expectation and the joy and the love that would be there.

I asked him that evening if I could get him anything, what would he want. He decided that he wanted some orange juice, so I went to town and got him some juice and took it up to his house. His wife was surprised because she said he hardly ever drank orange juice. He drank it, though, and said that it was good to the last drop!

The last few times that I visited Stewart, I could feel God's presence drawing closer. I knew his time to go home was approaching. I took a tape of hymns I have that was recorded by two members of our congregation. It is such beautiful worship music; it brings the peace and anointing of God right into the room. It is such an instrument, such a wonderful tool to use, to assist people through their pain and grief, and into death and into life eternal.

So I took that tape in and asked them to start playing it. I read scripture to Stewart and asked him if he could hear me to squeeze my hand. He kept squeezing my hand, and I kept talking to him.

A couple of days went by, and I got up to go to work one morning. I got ready to go, went out the door, and looked at my pager to see if I had been beeped; it hadn't gone off. But when I got to the end of my driveway, instead of turning left, I turned right. I found myself halfway up to his house before I even realized what I was doing. I was asking, "Okay, Lord, what is going on here? What am I doing? I am supposed to be going to the agency."

So I went on to Stewart's. When I pulled into the driveway, the family had the phone in their hands. They had been calling the parsonage and leaving messages and had been desperately trying to page me. They had been calling the wrong number, so my pager wasn't responding. They were astounded that I knew to come. I just smiled and said, "Well, God has a pager, too."

The family was quite upset and saying, "We don't think it is going to be long. Pop is dying." So I comforted them and reminded them of what he had waiting for him.

We went in to his room and put the music on. I shared with him, and he squeezed my hand. I told him that Jesus was drawing very close and for him to focus on the light, because only he would be able to see the light of Christ as he came into the room.

So I read from the book of Psalm to him and sang to him; I could just feel the peace and the presence and the anointing of God. His breaths became slower and slower, and he began to look at the ceiling. He closed his eyes, and there was such a look of peace that came over his face.

I knelt down beside his bed, and I said the Lord's Prayer. And as I was praying, I had my hand in his hand and one hand on his chest. As I finished and said "Amen," I felt the spirit leave the body; Jesus was there, and Jesus did what he does best. He picked Stewart up in His arms and carried him on to eternal life.

It was such a beautiful, peaceful moment that even the family was in awe from the love and joy in the midst of the grief that they were witnessing and experiencing.

So we went out into the living room, and we began to share stories about Stewart and his jokes. We laughed, and we cried. It was a beautiful going-home experience that left peace and comfort with the family, so they know that when this life is over, there is eternal life ahead for each of them and every believer and follower of Christ. This life is just a trial run, and even the most unrelenting illness can not deprive us of our eternal life when we keep our focus on our Savior. He can bring joy and encouragement to us, even in the darkest times!

"For this God is our God
for ever and ever:
he will be our guide even unto death."
Psalm 48:14

"I Love You, But I Don't Want To"

I had been trying to get ready to go to annual conference, and I stopped at the grocery story to pick up some things so my husband wouldn't starve while I was gone. I was leaving that day, and it had been a very busy day for me.

As I walked into the store, I saw this potted plant. The pot itself looked like two rocks with a golf ball stuck in a crevice of the rocks. I immediately thought of an elderly parishioner of mine who had been sick and recovering from surgery. I stood there for a moment, looking at it, thinking about getting it for her, but decided against it. Did I really have the time to visit her today?

I finished shopping and actually took my groceries out and put them in my car, and I knew by that time that I just had to get that flower. "Okay, Lord, I'll get the flower," I kind of whispered aloud.

So I went back in and got it. I got to my house, unloaded my groceries, put my meats and perishables away, and before I could even put the other things away, the Lord said to me, "You've **got** to go to Sarah **now**."

So I took the flower and headed off to see Sarah. She was staying with her daughter Susie at the time. I saw them sitting on the porch when I pulled up. I wanted to walk down quietly around the house and kind of surprise her, which I did. She hadn't seen or heard me when I pulled up. I gave her the flower, and she just loved it.

I told her if she could get that golf ball out of those rocks, then and only then could she teach me how to play golf. Even though she was in her eighties, she was still active and still loved the game. She was always teasing me about learning how to play. She said she knew she couldn't get that ball out of those rocks, but she could teach me how to play golf.

We sat there talking and had a delightful conversation. Her daughter Susie was there, her son-in-law Ralph was there, and Chris, another member of the family, came by. It was just delightful.

We sat there looking out over the field of corn. Sarah said, "Angie, I want you to look closely at that corn. Do you see the corn growing?"

I had to admit to her that I did not see the corn growing. So she said, "You really have to still yourself, and you really have to watch. But if you really focus, and you really clear your mind and heart, you'll see the corn growing."

About that time she said she needed to go in to use the restroom. She went in, and she suddenly started yelling. Her daughter and I ran in, and she came out of the bathroom. She was an ashen color. I helped her to the day bed and took her blood pressure; it was fine. Her pulse was a little fast, but not much. But she said she was really sick, sicker than she had ever been in her whole life.

At that point I told Susie that I thought she needed to call the ambulance, and she went to do that. Sarah would try to lie back, but she couldn't. It was too uncomfortable for her. I began to tell her, "Let's quote scripture together. So we quoted Psalm 23 and the Lord's Prayer. Then I began to sing hymns to her: "Amazing Grace" and "How Great Thou Art." She would sing parts of them with me---she was trying to appease me----but she was definitely very, very sick.

At this point, I thought about utilizing spiritual meditation to ease the pain. I sat down in front of her and asked her if she could focus on the most peaceful place that she could be with Jesus, where would it be? And she said, " It would be beside a bubbling stream. A clear bubbling stream, so clear that you could see the fish."

So I asked her if she could close her eyes and see herself sitting there, putting her feet in the bubbling water, feeling the peace of God. I asked her if she could look up through the field, could she see Jesus walking toward her.? She said that she could.

That was when I realized that she was dying because I could see the glow come into her face and she said, "Yes, I can see Him. Yes, I can see Jesus."

That's when I said, "Sarah, Sarah!" and she opened her eyes. I said, "Sarah, you have to fight to stay with us. Because if not, you are going to go be with the Lord."

She said, "I love you, but I don't want to." She leaned into me and I held her and sang to her. Then she did exactly what she wanted to do----she went to be with Jesus.

Sarah had served the Lord all of her life, and she was ready to go home! She didn't fear it, and she didn't fight it!

We often called Sarah the official greeter in our church. No one came through our church doors without getting a big hug, a warm smile, and a sincere invitation to come back. Those of us who knew Sarah best can easily picture her just inside the Pearly Gates, welcoming all who come to Glory-----grabbing each one to give a big hug, and flashing that beautiful smile---knowing that she is exactly where she wants to be!!

"But the path of the just
is as the shining light,
that shineth more and more
unto the perfect day."
Proverbs 4:18

"They Have To Let Me Go"

I had visited Ruth several times in the hospital. The first time was when she fell and broke her hip. I was with her after her surgery, when they had brought her back up to her room. Of course, she was in and out of consciousness. I sent the family down to eat, telling them that things would be okay, and they didn't need to be there.

I was sitting there reading the Bible to Ruth and saying the Lord's Prayer. As I was saying the Lord's Prayer, I got down on my knees beside her bed, and she was saying it with me. Then suddenly, she quit praying with me. I opened my eyes and looked up, and she wasn't breathing. I checked her pulse, and I couldn't find one.

I turned on the nurse's light and let out a yell for the nurse. When the nurse came in, she called a code. The room was immediately full of people, doing what they do best. They paged the family to come back up from the cafeteria----and we waited and we prayed.

I am not sure how long she was "gone," but she came back. I asked her about that experience, and she said that she had experienced life after death---that she had actually gone through the tunnel and into the light. She could hear the beautiful music, and she could feel the peace of God. But she said she couldn't stay because her family wasn't ready for her to leave yet. So she came back. She explained that Lawrie, her husband, was not ready to let her go, and he would not be alright without her. His name was Lawrence, but her name for him was Lawrie, and they were truly devoted to each other-----joined in mind and in spirit.

I am not sure how much time passed, maybe a year or a year and a half, when the next episode in the hospital occurred. This time it was congestive heart failure. I went to visit her, and we had quite a little visit. She told me how she wanted her funeral service to be---that she wanted it to be a worship service. She wanted God to be praised and to have a lot of scripture and testimonies.

As we were sharing, one of the Catholic sisters came into the room, and Ruth introduced us. She introduced me as her minister, and we had a very nice visit as we shared our ministries and our love for the Lord together. As we were sitting there, the nurse came into the room and asked Ruth what denomination she was. Without a moment's hesitation, she replied, "Christian," and we both laughed.

The nurse said, "I know you are Christian, but you have to be a denomination."

Ruth and I looked at each other and smiled. At our union-yoked church, consisting of Presbyterian **and** Methodist, we just call ourselves Christians. It's because of the love and example that Christ set for us that we worship and live as just that-----Christians. Ruth, understanding that the nurse had a task to accomplish, explained our unusual congregation. I, being the Methodist minister, hold worship services on the second and fourth Sundays. The Presbyterian minister leads worship on the first and third Sundays. Our Sunday school combines each Sunday. But most of the congregation just comes each Sunday to worship with our church family, regardless of the minister bringing the Word that day.

So Ruth explained, "Well, I guess I am a Presbyterian. But I would like to introduce you to my little United Methodist minister here."

So after that, I called Ruth a "Prebymethodist." After the nurse left the room, she said, "You've got one to tease me on now. Here I am, patting your hand, and I know you are a Methodist. And I told them to write down Presbyterian. I hope you don't get mad."

I said, "Of course not, but I will tease you about this, you little Presbymethodist."

Not too long after that, the doctors decided that for Ruth to have quality of life and be blessed with a few more years, she would have to go on to another hospital and have valve replacement surgery to repair her heart.

Well, Ruth went on to Charlottesville, Virginia, and had the surgery. Shortly after she had the surgery, I went to the hospital to visit Ruth, and she was anxious to see me. Her voice was so weak that I had to put ice chips in her mouth so she could say just a few words. Then I'd have to put a few more ice chips in her mouth, and she would say a few more words.

She made me promise to go out and talk with the family and explain to them that they needed to let her go. So I made that promise to her, and we prayed together. She confided in me that during the surgery she had left her body again, and that she had gotten even closer to God. She had gone through the tunnel, into the light, and out into this beautiful, beautiful meadow or pasture where she could see this stream of water running through----like the beautiful Jordan.

She had been able to see her beautiful Ethel, her daughter who had died of cancer years before and her beloved son Larry, who as a teenager had been killed in a motorcycle accident. She knew it was time to stay there, to be with God and to be with them. Her time here was well spent, but it was close to being over. And she said, "But I just need for them to let me go----for them to understand that it is time for me to go."

So I went out, and I went into the waiting room. I talked to the family about what Ruth had shared, and I told Lawrie that sometimes we---all of us--- have to sacrifice. Sometimes we have to let the true love of our life go on-----to be with God----and receive the benefits of that healing.

He said he understood. It had been a very difficult time for everyone. Ruth had come out of this surgery with a very rare, very odd effect---she had become paralyzed from the neck down. She made light of it and made jokes of it. She said they could stick her toes and feet with needles and things and not worry--- she wouldn't kick them. She was very humorous and jolly and praiseful the entire time. She knew, though, that the paralysis was permanent, and she would never recover the use of her body. I watched as Lawrie was faced with perhaps the greatest test of his love for his beloved Ruth. I know that he thought about her request carefully and asked the Lord's help in what to do.

Lawrie went into the room with me, and he told Ruth that it was okay for her to go on to be with God.

He said that he released her, and he lifted his hands toward heaven and said, "I release you to go be with God." And each of the daughters did the same.

My parishioner friend Susie was with me. Susie's mom Sarah, who had passed away earlier, was a great friend of Ruth's, and Ruth was asking to speak to Susie. When Susie came in, Ruth said to her, "Susie, I've seen Sarah, and I've been talking to her. She wants you to know that she is praying for you." And then she said, "Please pray for Angie and Rocky. Always pray earnestly for them."

It was God's plan that Susie be with me and receive those words, as well as for me to be there that day to help this family. We visited as much as we could, then we left and came on home. Three days later, as I was doing an Easter egg hunt with the residents from the agency, I got word that she was near death and the family was asking everyone in the church to pray. So I gathered some of the other parishioners who were there with me from the church together, we joined hands in a circle, and we prayed that her journey to be with Jesus be peaceful and joyous. We received word shortly after that she had indeed gone to be with Jesus, and that her passing was about the same time that we had gathered in prayer after receiving the word of her condition. The family was all around her bed, praying her home when her time came.

I can just imagine the joy she experienced as she crossed over and did indeed stay and receive the total restoration of her body and a total healing that we all yearn for. I can only imagine the reunion that occurred as she finally joined her loved ones who had gone before her, and when she finally walked into the arms of Jesus, whom she had loved and served all of her life. But she stayed long enough to prepare her family for her journey so they could, indeed, willingly let her go to her home in Glory and wait for them there.

"For ye shall go out with joy,
and be led forth with peace:
the mountains and the hills shall break forth before you into singing,
and all the trees of the field shall clap their hands."
Isaiah 55:12

"I Am Willing, Lord, But I Am Not Perfect"

One of the major struggles that I have had in my ministry is public speaking. I struggle with that every time I get into the pulpit. This goes back to my sickness, I am sure, and being out of school so much of what I call the primary years where the vocabulary skills are developed and the English and grammar is taught and all that formation is happening. Also, I was raised in a Dutch-German culture, where the dialect I learned as a child and was exposed to was somewhat different than most folks. I also have had a little bit of a stammer in my voice. So a combination of all of that has made me a little uncomfortable in the pulpit.

As I struggle with this, God reminds me that in the Old Testament He spoke to Balaam through his donkey. God has revealed to me that if we are obedient, He can and will speak through us.

I know that there is not a Sunday that goes by that God does not speak through me. I go into the pastor's study and I pray and I pray and I pray, "Yes, Oh God, please. I have studied, and I have prepared. I have read Your word; I have listened for discernment of Your word. Please give me the words and the message that I need today to touch their hearts and bring them to You." Then the minute that I step behind that pulpit, I feel this anointing come down upon my body, and it is just a covering. It is a warmth.

I feel myself become free in Him as I allow Him to use me as that vessel to share His word and His love with His children. And so I encourage **everyone** to be willing and be obedient.

God is speaking to hearts around the world, but people are waiting for the day when they are perfect, when they have received all their education so they can get every sentence right, every verb tense right. But God is just wanting people to say, "Yes, Lord, use me." We need to remember that God uses the humble, and I think God uses the meek to teach the wise. That goes along with the Sermon on the Mount. We have to be willing to let God use our gifts and abilities because he even spoke through a donkey. Anybody who is willing, God will bless and use as an instrument for Himself.

"These things I have spoken unto you,
that in me ye might have peace.
In the world ye shall have tribulation,
but be of good cheer;
I have overcome the world."
John 16:33

"Seeding Cherries And Sorting Fears"

It was a time in my life when, as a young adult, I had re-dedicated my life to Christ. I wanted to be able to do things perfectly in God's eyes. I wanted to live a **perfect** life and be perfect for the Lord. It seemed like the harder I tried to go through each day and have the best attitude and the best actions and the best for everybody that I came into contact with, the worse it became. It seemed to me that I kept falling short of the mark. I was getting really discouraged with myself.

So one evening I went to Rev. Kile's, my spiritual mentor's, house. I pulled up into his driveway. He was sitting out under a tree, and he was seeding cherries. As I walked over, and he could see that I was very distressed. It was as if my face was covered with gloom and doom, and he said, "Have a seat. Fetch a bowl, and help me seed some cherries, and we'll talk about life."

So he gave me a bowl of cherries, and I began seeding them. He asked me to share what was on my heart. I did, and I said, "You know, I really want to do this right. I really want to be a good Christian, and I really want to do my best for God. But I just can't do it; I just can't be it. I keep falling short."

He didn't laugh at me or anything. He took me very seriously. He looked at me for a moment or two, then he began to teach me---quietly, softly, patiently—

as I imagine Jesus often did. His conversation went like this:

"You see these cherries, Angie. We---you and I and all of us—we are a lot like them. When we are ripe for the working of God----when it is time----He'll call. Just like when we picked these cherries. But even after they are picked, they aren't ready to use. They have to go through a process. Any time we fail, we go through a process, too. We need to open our heart and say, 'God, I messed up.' Just like taking the seed out of this cherry. It will be delicious when we are finished. Let God open up your heart and take all the seeds out---all the pain and fear and indecision and everything. God takes them out and makes us more fruitful. All we need to do is ask and seek Him. By the time He's finished with us, we are just what He wants us to be. Just like these cherries. We have many uses for them, but we have to get them ready first. God has many uses for us, but we have to go through the process and be ready first. We are not ready for use when we are first picked. He makes us fruitful and just right for the use He has chosen for us."

He said, "Angie, the closing of each day is like seeding these cherries. You just have to take the worst out of the day and just give it to God and ask God to forgive and know that His great mercy and grace covers that. We learn from those times when we fall short, but there is no perfect person." In 1 John, the Bible says that the only perfect person was Christ Jesus, and he was the supreme sacrifice for each and every one of us.

We talked about life, as we sat there seeding those cherries. I poured out my heart, and he listened.

I realized that it was like he said, just like those cherries. You take the pit out of the cherries, and the pit is important. It is actually the seed, and it makes it grow. It is just like our trials and our shortcomings. It is because of those that we are forced to grow in our Christian faith. Yes, we want to remove those. We want to take those out each and every day. That makes us more fruitful in our ministry, more fruitful in our Christian walk.

Our lives are just like those cherries. Once we pitted them, they were excellent for cobblers and pies. It just doesn't happen automatically. It takes work.

We were out there for an hour or two, just pitting cherries and talking about life. He taught me there, sitting under the tree, very much as I imagine Jesus did when he was teaching his followers. Like any mentor, Rev. Kile has had a tremendous influence on my life and my ministry. He presided over the funeral services of both my mother and my father, and he stayed in touch with me and helped me through some very, very difficult times in my life. He just continued to offer support and spiritual guidance, and he invited me to attend a revival at his church.

As a young person searching for meaning in my life, I remember feeling the tremendous love of God surrounding me when I walked into his church. He asked me to give a testimony and share as part of the service. When I did, I felt so blessed and so blanketed by the love in the church that I felt like I had to sing---- and I did. Just after that he asked me to be lay speaker, and I began to feel the real calling to the ministry. At first I really didn't want the call. I didn't feel worthy or capable. He greatly encouraged me in my ministry, though. I would speak for him at revivals, and I was a lay speaker in his church. He cultivated that through his encouragement of who and what I could be in Christ if I would just allow God and the Holy Spirit to lead me. I praise God for that mentor and the love that was shown to me through Rev. Kile and his wife, Ruth.

I have learned that as we go through life each day, we constantly seed and sort. And if we continue to do so----if we continue to nurture our faith-----the harvest will be bountiful and great!!

"For I the Lord thy God will hold thy right hand,
saying unto thee,
Fear not; I will help thee."
Isaiah 41:13

"We Are Called To Help, Not To Judge"

If we do try to help others, as God commands us to do, sometimes we are misled. But God still calls us to try to help others in need.

When I first came to Burlington, I had to have gall bladder surgery right away. It was the week of vacation Bible school, and I was determined to be there and to spend time with the children. I would spend the day resting. Later in the evening I would go over to be with the children . I wanted to get to know the people in my new charge.

I remember there was a man who knocked on my door one day during that week. He said he was in need and was hitchhiking. He needed food and something to drink.

For safety reasons, I asked him to sit out on the stoop, and I would bring him out something. So I fixed him a cold drink and took it out to him with some fruit that I had. I made some calls to arrange a place to stay for him. I fixed him a sandwich and some chips--- like a picnic type lunch and went back down the steps again, knowing that I was not supposed to be climbing stairs so soon after my surgery. But I believed that this man had a need, and I was doing my best to meet that need.

I learned that sometimes when we give, people have motivations that are wrong. I gave him his food that day, and he asked for money. I honestly could not give him money, but I promised him that there was a room waiting for him just a couple of miles down the road. I told him that if he walked out to the end of the road, he could catch a ride with some of my colleagues as they left work. Several would be driving where he would need to go----where his room was waiting for him.

He became angry at that. He took his food and threw it across the yard. He said some well-chosen words and left. I prayed for him as he stormed away, asking that God would relieve his anger and meet his needs as only He could. He did go stay in the room, though, because I got the bill for it later in the mail. So I know that in that way he was blessed.

But the scripture says that we need to give to strangers and those in need. We are supposed to do what we can. Sometimes it is accepted, and sometimes it is not. But we need to be obedient to do what we can.

Another time this kind of incident happened was during Mother's Day. There was a lady who came and knocked on the church door. It was after church, and she was in need of a room and had her mind absolutely set to have a Mother's Day buffet. She was going to eat at a Mother's Day buffet because she was a mother and had two sons and that was what she wanted to do. So, again, I tried to be obedient to God's word and offer a helping hand to her.

I sent her off with my husband to the nearest store. He bought her a phone card and some snacks, and I made the necessary calls to make sure she had a place to stay in the next town. Things were closer there. There were more stores, and she could walk to the restaurants in town.

My husband and I were supposed to be meeting his mother for Mother's Day, but this lady had greatly changed our plans. We called and told my mother-in-law that we would be late. We explained that we needed to help this individual, and my mother-in-law understood. So we drove our guest to the next town and took her to two or three restaurants, but she refused to eat at each of them because they didn't have a buffet----and that is what she definitely had in mind that she would have.

We finally took her to her room, but she wouldn't stay because she wanted us to take her to **another** restaurant to try the buffet. At this point we were beginning to feel like we wouldn't be able to help her-----that she would not accept the help we offered. As we were driving around, we saw a little restaurant that had a buffet sign in the window. We told her that we really needed to go because we were late with our own plans, and we had spent several hours getting her situated. By then I was too hungry to wait until I got to my mother-in-law's because that was an hour and a half away, so we stopped to grab a sandwich. When we did, there sat our lady friend again.

She carried a walkman with her the whole time and kept going on and on about calling her sons so they could wish her a happy Mother's Day. Of course, my husband had also helped meet that need by buying her a phone card.

Did she have a genuine need, or did she use us for her gain? You never know. Should I have turned her away because I doubted her? I think not. God says that we should never turn a stranger in need away. You never know what seeds you plant. So we do what we can do with each and every day. We know that God will take that effort and add to it, and it will suffice for those who need it.

"Be not forgetful to entertain strangers:
for thereby some have entertained angels unawares."
Hebrews 13: 2

"God Is Calling, But Are You Listening?"

I ask **you** now, "Is your container in life half empty or half full?" Do you concentrate on what you **don't have**, or do you recognize the blessings you **do have**?

When God is trying to reach out to you, are you quiet and obedient and open to Him----listening? Or are you in such a hurry to find your own answer that His plan for you is unseen?

I pray that the stories God has given me to share with you will remind you, as they continue to remind me, that God is anxious to be the center of all our lives----the lives of everyday, common people just like you and me. We don't have to be rich and famous, gifted and entertaining, or physically strong and free of infirmities. He loves and accepts all of us because He created us exactly as He wants us. He wants to comfort us, heal us, love us, and lead us---but we must submit our will to Him and accept His plan in our lives.

Would you let your pager go unanswered? Would you let your phone ring constantly and refuse to answer? Would you ignore the plea of a child, a friend, or another loved one as they cry out to you for help? I think not. But then why do we ignore God when He tries to reach out to us? Why do we ignore Him when He tries to help us?

Let us be wise and still ourselves before God just a few minutes each day, praying and seeking Him, and really listen to what He is saying to us. Let us remind ourselves that what He has for us is far better than we could plan or design for ourselves. If we totally accept God and His will in our lives, we can not even debate whether our vessels are half empty or half full-----our cups will be brimming with blessings only He can provide.

As each of us accepts Jesus as our Lord and Savior, we can truly say, "My cup runneth over."

God is calling. Are you listening?

Psalm 23
The Lord is my shepherd;
I shall not want.
He maketh me to lie down in green pastures:
he leadeth me beside the still waters.
He restoreth my soul;
he leadeth me in paths of righteousness for his name's sake.
Yea, though I walk through the valley of the shadow of death,
I will fear no evil:
for thou art with me;
thy rod and thy staff they comfort me.
Thou preparest a table before me
in the presence of mine enemies:
thou anointest my head with oil:
my cup runneth over.
Surely goodness and mercy shall follow me
all the days of my life:
and I will dwell in the house of the Lord forever.

Rev. Angela Cosner is an ordained United Methodist minister of the West Virginia Annual Conference, having studied Christian theology at Duke University in Durham, NC. She is pastor of the Burlington United Methodist Church in Burlington, WV. She also serves as campus chaplain and director in charge of the Spiritual Life Program of the Burlington United Methodist Family Services, a residential treatment facility for at-risk youth.

Angela is also a registered nurse. She earned her associate degree from Davis and Elkins College in Elkins, WV, and later received her bachelor's degree from West Virginia University. She is currently pursuing her master's degree in mental health counseling from Marshall University.

Pastor Angie is an active participant in the United Methodist Association, a national organization, and has been asked to serve as chaplain of the Order of Good Shepherd Task Force for that organization. She receives requests to serve as a resource person from people across the country to share materials, advice, and models for implementation of programs for at-risk youth. She also provides mentorship for other chaplains who are modeling and implementing programs similar to Burlington's spiritual life program.

Angela is a strong advocate of holistic health. She believes that total healing comes only through treatment of the physical, spiritual, and emotional needs. Pastor Angie feels led to educate people about holistic health care and to develop curriculum materials for at-risk youth.

Take time to enjoy God's gifts to us.

Simple Pleasures

And Great Joys

"Delight thyself also in the Lord;
and he shall give thee
the desires of thine heart."

Psalm 37:4

Kathy Johnson is a language arts teacher with nearly 25 years experience. A freelance writer, she has published numerous articles in national magazines and newspapers. She holds a master's degree in communication studies from West Virginia University in Morgantown, WV, where she has done extensive post-graduate work. She has two children and resides with her husband Bill ---also a teacher---in Burlington, WV, where they are both very active in their church.

How to Order

Additional copies of this book are always available from the authors, local book stores, Baker and Taylor Distributors, or at the following:

Main Street Books
60 N. Main St.
Keyser, WV 26726
(304) 788-3043

Have comments or questions? Contact the authors at

Rev. Angela Cosner
P.O. Box 57
Burlington, WV 26710

Kathy Johnson
Rt. 2 Box 8C
Burlington, WV 26710

Copies may also be ordered online at
mcclainprinting.com
amazon.com
barnesandnoble.com
waldenbooks
books-a-million

You may reach the authors at the above addresses, or email us at
angelacosner@hotmail.com
kejohnson@citlink.net

"Blessed be the Lord,
who daily loadeth us with benefits,
even the God of our Salvation."
Psalm 68:19